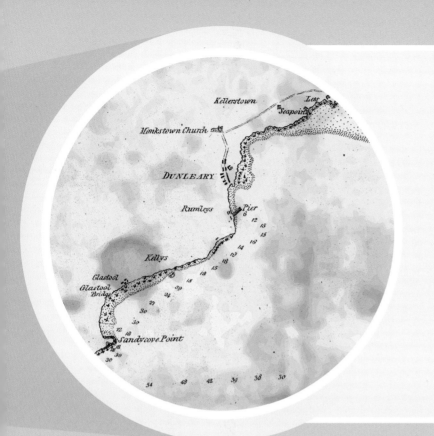

The southern shore of Dublin Bay was rocky and dangerous to shipping. Very few people lived between Dalkey and Dublin, and Dunleary was a poor fishing village where the Monkstown stream entered the sea. Monkstown Church is also marked. The original pier built in 1767 can be seen. This pier still guards the Coal Harbour today. Kellys near Glastool (Glasthule) may have been a tavern. It marks the approximate point where the East Pier was built.

PROPOSED HARBOUR

This was an early proposal for a harbour including the pier of 1767. It was published in a pamphlet by A Seaman, presumed to be Richard Toutcher, in 1811.

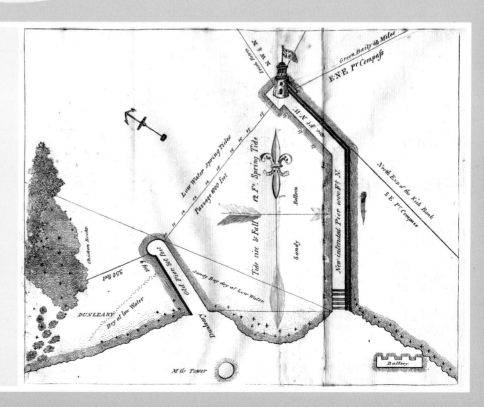

Blackrock Education Centre
Ionad Oideachais na Carraige Duibhe

Blackrock Education Centre 2018

ISBN 978-0-9563141-9-2

Published by Blackrock Education Centre in collaboration with Dún Laoghaire Harbour Company, to mark the bicentenary of Dún Laoghaire Harbour.

Blackrock Education Centre, Kill Avenue, Dún Laoghaire, Co. Dublin, A96 EW01.

becbooks@blackrockec.ie/ www.becpublishing.com

Blackrock Education Centre is an agency of the Department of Education and Skills.

First published 2018.

Author
Séamus Cannon, with Gráinne O'Malley and Colin Scudds

Editor
Gráinne O'Malley

Graphic Design, Illustration and Formatting
Eliane Pearce
contact@elianepearce.com
www.elianepearce.com

Cover Design
Eliane Pearce

Cover image
'You'd be filled with Wonder' is a line from a contemporary ballad at the time of the 1821 visit of King George IV to Kingstown Harbour (now Dún Laoghaire). The painting is of a ketch called the *Iris.* It was used by members of the Dublin Sketching Club during the late nineteenth and early twentieth century to sail out into Dublin Bay and beyond, to sketch and paint seascapes.
The painting is used by kind permission of artist **Aidan Hickey.**

"You'd be Filled with Wonder"

The story of

Dún Laoghaire Harbour

1817 – 2017

Séamus Cannon
with Gráinne O'Malley and Colin Scudds

This book is dedicated to the memory of Captain Richard Toutcher, a forgotten hero. Without him, there would have been no harbour at Dún Laoghaire.

To Peggy and Connie; Eoin and Lia,
the latest generation to delight in his wonderful creation.

Foreword | Blackrock Education Centre

Blackrock Education Centre is delighted to collaborate with Dún Laoghaire Harbour Company in bringing the story of the harbour to a wider audience. I welcome this opportunity to encourage a new generation to learn about and to take pride in this wonderful creation. Dún Laoghaire Harbour was a sensational development at the time of its construction and through the stories in this book we consider the imagination and courage of those responsible. It is hard to imagine today how perilous sea travel was in the age of sail and how vital the harbour was in saving lives.

We are also delighted to acknowledge the collaboration of the Dún Laoghaire Historical Society, the National Maritime Museum and the DLR LexIcon in promoting a sense of our past to a new generation. We hope that our book will add to the enjoyment of our harbour by young people and by the general public alike.

Dr Susan Gibney, *Director, Blackrock Education Centre.*

Foreword | Dún Laoghaire Harbour Company

Dún Laoghaire Harbour is widely recognised as one of the finest man-made harbours in the world. It is also a unique architectural heritage site of national and international importance. In May 2017, the harbour celebrated its Bicentenary with a visit from Uachtarán Na hÉireann, Michael D. Higgins.

It is important to give a special mention to Captain Richard Toutcher, a Norwegian national who spearheaded the plan to create an asylum harbour in Dublin Bay. Without Captain Toutcher, we would not enjoy the public amenity that we have today.

The directors and staff of Dún Laoghaire Harbour Company, together with the members of the Harbour Bicentenary Steering Group, would like to thank Blackrock Education Centre and Dr Séamus Cannon for the beautiful manner in which many classic harbour tales have been told.

Gerry Dunne, *CEO Dún Laoghaire Harbour Company.*

Contents

A Tragic Shipwreck

Dún Laoghaire harbour had its origin in a terrible tragedy over 200 years ago.

It happened in 1807, when Britain was at war with France. On the night of November 18th, two ships set sail from Dublin port. There were hundreds of people on board – soldiers and their families including 29 children – all bound for the war. Many of the soldiers were Irishmen, as Ireland was then part of the United Kingdom. The ships, the *Prince of Wales* and the *Rochdale,* caught the wind and made their way towards the open bay.

But they never reached their final destination.

At that time, all ships were powered by sail and were at the mercy of the wind and tide. Dublin Bay was already known to be very dangerous and was the scene of many shipwrecks. This was because sandbanks in the bay made it difficult for ships to enter Dublin harbour, except at high tide. If a ship was caught in a storm in the open bay, there was no shelter.

As the two ships set out, a gale sprang up and the winds gathered force as they made their way out into Dublin Bay. Soon conditions worsened and driving snow made it difficult for the crews to navigate. They tried to drop anchor, but the storm was so fierce that the cables snapped. Now they were in great danger. There was no shelter in the open bay but they couldn't get back to harbour. The *Prince of Wales* struggled as far as Bray Head but it was blown back to Dublin Bay. High waves and wind carried it closer and closer to the jagged coastline. Sadly, the ship was wrecked on the rocks at Blackrock, a short distance from Dún Laoghaire. More than a hundred lives were lost. The captain and crew, with a small number of others, survived by escaping in a small boat but almost all the soldiers were lost. It was alleged that they had been locked below deck.

The fate of the *Rochdale* was even more tragic. She was driven along the coast by the fierce storm. People watched on the shore, horrified and helpless, as the ship struggled. They were so close that they could hear the cries of the terrified passengers. The crew fired muskets to attract attention,

"A great part of the beach from Dunleary to the Rock was covered yesterday morning with the bodies of the victims who suffered; but Seapoint… has been a scene of horror indescribable".

The Freeman's Journal, 1807

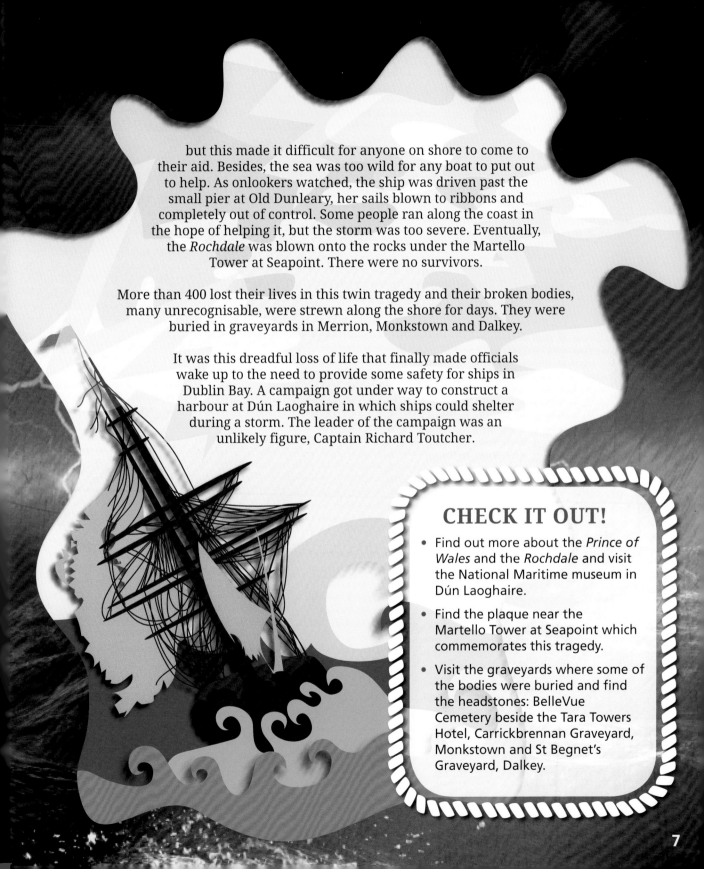

but this made it difficult for anyone on shore to come to their aid. Besides, the sea was too wild for any boat to put out to help. As onlookers watched, the ship was driven past the small pier at Old Dunleary, her sails blown to ribbons and completely out of control. Some people ran along the coast in the hope of helping it, but the storm was too severe. Eventually, the *Rochdale* was blown onto the rocks under the Martello Tower at Seapoint. There were no survivors.

More than 400 lost their lives in this twin tragedy and their broken bodies, many unrecognisable, were strewn along the shore for days. They were buried in graveyards in Merrion, Monkstown and Dalkey.

It was this dreadful loss of life that finally made officials wake up to the need to provide some safety for ships in Dublin Bay. A campaign got under way to construct a harbour at Dún Laoghaire in which ships could shelter during a storm. The leader of the campaign was an unlikely figure, Captain Richard Toutcher.

CHECK IT OUT!

- Find out more about the *Prince of Wales* and the *Rochdale* and visit the National Maritime museum in Dún Laoghaire.

- Find the plaque near the Martello Tower at Seapoint which commemorates this tragedy.

- Visit the graveyards where some of the bodies were buried and find the headstones: BelleVue Cemetery beside the Tara Towers Hotel, Carrickbrennan Graveyard, Monkstown and St Begnet's Graveyard, Dalkey.

A Forgotten Hero

Out of the tragic events of 1807 came some good. People were shocked by the great loss of life and many called for a safe harbour in Dublin Bay. Without Captain Richard Toutcher, however, it might never have been built.

Toutcher was Norwegian but had been living in Dublin for many years. He was a ship's captain and had his own shipbroking business. He believed passionately and stubbornly that a harbour should be built in Dún Laoghaire. Most of his life – and his own money – would be devoted to making this happen.

For some time, there had been calls for a "harbour of refuge" in Dublin, especially for ships caught in storms within the bay. Since Viking days, Dublin had always been the most important port in Ireland. But ships were now bigger and the entrance to the port was becoming more silted up with sandbanks, making it dangerous at low tide. Dublin Bay had a reputation as a graveyard for ships and the 1807 tragedy made it clear – something had to be done. But what?

There were very mixed views. In 1807, work had already started on a new harbour at Howth. But Toutcher protested that the Howth harbour would never do the job and he was proven to be right, as the harbour quickly filled with mud and sand. He called for a harbour at the other side of Dublin Bay, where the water was deeper. Dunleary had a small pier, but it dried out at low tide. He chose a site further east along the coast where Dún Laoghaire is today. It is hard to believe that, in those days, this shoreline was wild and empty. Blackrock was already a fashionable seaside resort and Dalkey had been an important harbour since the Middle Ages. But very few people lived in the rocky area between.

This, Toutcher believed, was where the new harbour had to be.

When the 1807 tragedy struck, Richard Toutcher sprang into action. He held a public meeting in Monkstown Church in 1808 and got the backing of many public figures for his new harbour. He wrote to other important people and he was also believed to be the author of a very influential publication written anonymously by 'A Seaman'. It argued that Dún Laoghaire was "the only spot where an harbour can be built with safety and advantage". His campaign led to an Act of Parliament authorising the building of a harbour.

Toutcher not only campaigned for the harbour, he did something very significant. He knew that a harbour would need large amounts of granite stone but landowners were likely to charge high sums. At his own expense, he took out a lease of ten acres on Dalkey Hill to quarry granite. He then provided the granite

CONSIDERATIONS

ON

THE NECESSITY AND IMPORTANCE

OF

AN ASYLUM PORT,

ROYAL IRISH ACADEMY

HALIDAY COLLECTION

THE BAY OF DUBLIN:

INCLUDING

REMARKS ON THE HARBOUR

ERECTING AT

HOWTH;

AND THAT

(WHICH IS THE OBJECT OF VARIOUS PETITIONS)

PROPOSED FOR

DUNLEARY.

BY A SEAMAN.

another Edition pp 66 v 24, IV

DUBLIN:

Printed and published by J. BULL, No. 10, Strand-Street.—For the AUTHOR.

1811.

to the Harbour Commissioners free of charge. This was a huge sacrifice. It was also a huge public saving (a staggering £240,000 in those times), one that made the harbour possible.

His original plan had been to build a single pier, the East Pier, with a bend towards the North West. Others argued that it would quickly silt up. John Rennie, chief engineer for the harbour, recommended a second pier and this was eventually agreed. With some changes in detail, this was to become the harbour we know today.

For many years, Richard Toutcher fought for a harbour in Dún Laoghaire and he won. But he neglected his own business, debts built up and he had to ask the government for compensation. It was refused and he died a bankrupt. Ten years after the 1807 shipwrecks, on May 31, 1817, the Lord Lieutenant laid the foundation stone, for the new harbour. Among the names inscribed on it, the name Richard Toutcher is not to be found. Yet he was responsible, more than anyone else, for the construction of the harbour and for the town which grew up around it. His great contribution was never recognised in his own lifetime, which was a great injustice.

He is indeed a forgotten hero.

CHECK IT OUT!

- Find out what you can about Captain Richard Toutcher.
- Check the names on the harbour foundation stone under the George IV memorial.
- Look up the 1811 campaign pamphlet, by "A Seaman". Study the early map of Dublin Bay to see the risks.

"An Able and Intelligent Engineer"

This was how John Rennie was described when he was appointed chief engineer for Dún Laoghaire harbour in 1815. In fact, he was one of the greatest engineers of his time - and he needed to be.

He was about to build the largest man-made harbour in the world.

Rennie was born in Scotland, the son of a farmer, and as a young boy he showed a great interest in engineering. In his early years, he worked as a mechanical engineer, designing machinery for milling grain. By 1815 he was already famous for his success in designing and building canals, bridges and harbours across Britain. His best-known work was probably Waterloo Bridge in London. In 1817, he completed Howth harbour in Ireland and he was also involved in building the Royal Canal.

When he took on the new harbour, Rennie had the benefit of a survey of Dublin Bay by Captain Bligh in 1800. Bligh was, of course, famous as the captain of the *Bounty* on which there was a mutiny some years earlier. Rennie agreed that the best place to build a harbour was a little over a kilometre east of the fishing village of Dunleary. He later argued that there should be two piers, as a single pier would cause a build-up of sand. A West Pier was then added to the plans. Rennie appointed another Scot, John Aird, as the site engineer and both names can be seen on the George IV memorial. When Rennie died in 1821, his son (also John) took over.

It is hard to realise how enormous this project was. The combined length of both piers in Dún Laoghaire is 2.8km. The bottom of each pier is 90 metres wide and the piers stand 15 metres above the sea bed. Every rock you see was carved by hand.

It took 36 years to build the harbour, from 1817 until 1853 when the Traders' Wharf was finished. The final design was not quite what Rennie had planned. He had wanted a narrow mouth at the harbour entrance to provide more shelter. But the Royal Navy overruled this as they needed a wider entrance for their ships.

Rennie's first task was to secure a supply of stone for the massive building project. Remember that stone, iron and wood were the only building materials at that time. Because Richard Toutcher had bought the rights to quarry at Dalkey Hill, there was a free supply of granite stone. But the stone had to be quarried and carried over three kilometers to the sea. Rennie designed a very novel railway which linked the quarry to the harbour construction site.

The Diving Bell

John Rennie was ahead of his time in many ways, including the use of a diving bell. His bell allowed up to six men to work for hours under the water. It was made of cast iron with a leather pipe to the surface. Air was pumped by hand into the submerged bell by men on the surface. It weighed 5 tons and could also carry large stone blocks under water.

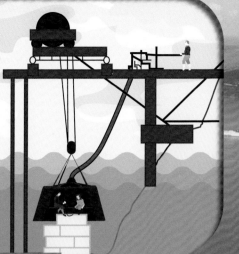

Building on the Sea Bed

Most of Dún Laoghaire harbour is under water. Like the tip of an iceberg, what we see is only a small part of a vast structure. The foundations stretch 7.3 metres below the low tide mark! But how did Rennie build his piers in the middle of the sea? He used a technique called "à pierre perdue". Loose rock was tipped onto the seabed and the wave movement built it into piles. The top was then "paved" with large stones wedged and cemented together.

"...the many splendid and useful works by which under his superintending genius England, Scotland and Ireland have been adorned."

Epitaph on John Rennie's gravestone

CHECK IT OUT!

- Find out more about John Rennie's other amazing engineering designs.
- Spot the bollard on the East Pier which was originally a cannon.
- Visit the diving bell on Sir John Rogerson's Quay, Dublin.

Moving a Hill by Rail

By 1820, Dalkey Hill was a hive of industry. Every day, rock blasting explosions filled the air. Trucks rattled up and down the slopes. Hundreds of labourers worked in the quarry and farmers complained about the disruption and noise. There was a sense of urgency - a flow of granite was needed to feed the new harbour project. Thanks to Richard Toutcher, the granite was available free of charge but it travelled quite a distance. The new East Pier was, after all, 3.5km away.

How did they transport the stone from hill to sea?

Rennie's solution was a railway track, an astonishing feat of engineering. Wagons laden with stone were hauled along a track from the quarry to the new piers. Each wagon carried between five and six tonnes of stone and an average of 322 wagons a day rattled down Dalkey Hill. The heavy wagons were lowered down the steep part of Dalkey Hill on chains. The chains passed around a pair of large friction wheels, which made sure that the wagons did not run too quickly. As the stone-filled wagons moved down the hill, their weight pulled the empty wagons up a second track. Once the wagons reached flat ground, horses were hitched up and pulled them the rest of the way. As the harbour extended, the railway track ran alongside it, bringing stone to the outermost tips of the piers.

The route created for this railway still survives today and is known as The Metals.

The contractor for quarrying and supplying stone was George Smith, who gave his name to Smith's cottages in Glenageary and to Newtownsmith. As many as 690 labourers at a time worked in the quarry during the building of the harbour. They included quarrymen, wagon drivers, machine operators, carpenters, blacksmiths and maintenance men. As well as quarrying the stone, they also had to maintain the machinery and the trackway and attend to the horses.

It was hard work. People worked six days or even six and a half. All workmen had to sign a contract that forbade them from joining a union, but there was a general strike in 1826 which lasted a month. However, the men were driven back to work. The workers were reasonably well paid by the standards of the time and it was steady work. But in bad weather, when they couldn't work, they were not paid at all!

The work was also dangerous, particularly in the quarry. Men worked in teams of three. One man held a large drilling chisel while the other two struck it in turn with sledgehammers with all their might. As the hole deepened, the chisel holder kept turning the chisel to clear the hole. The hole was then packed with gunpowder and an explosion was set off. You can still see the chisel holes in the quarry and on stone on the piers. The rocks were then broken down further for transportation in the wagons.

Dreadfully Mangled

Serious injury was common. A crane collapsed on James Weldon and "so dreadfully mangled him as to occasion his death the same day". Michael Bryon of Monkstown lost both his legs in 1828 when a loaded truck went over him. He was supplied with artificial legs.

"Success attend each honest heart,
The plumber and mason and worthy labourer,
For towards each poor man he nobly did his part."

From the 19th century ballad, The Beauties of Kingstown.

CHECK IT OUT!

- The Metals is now a popular walking and cycling route. Take the opportunity to explore it.

- Read *The Metals* by Rob Goodbody.

- Study the stones on the piers and in the quarry. Can you find chisel marks made by the quarrymen?

Working and Living Conditions

In 1826, the Reverend Charles Lindsay complained about the "lawless violence" on Dalkey Commons. People, he said, were living in houses "free of rent, free of tithes and free of taxes." These were the labourers who had flocked with their families to work on the new harbour. Many of them built their own makeshift huts and stone cabins near the quarry, in the area where Sorrento Road and Coliemore Road are today. They were squatters and conditions were often miserable. They had no sanitation, the only water came from local springs and there were often outbreaks of deadly typhus and cholera.

Life was difficult, but they put up with conditions because there was work.

The harbour was, after all, the biggest building project in Ireland at that time. The workers came from all parts of Ireland and also from Scotland. There were skilled craftsmen, unskilled labourers and soldiers returned home after the defeat of Napoleon at Waterloo. There were also people affected by the famine of 1816, when the harvest failed. The harbour offered hope to many and a chance to survive. In 1823, some 690 men worked in the quarry and 129 were employed at the harbour site. When the railway was built in 1834, linking the harbour to Dublin, there was a new surge in demand for workers.

The work paid quite well. In the early days, men were not paid in cash but with tickets which could be cashed with a publican or shopkeeper. This led to abuse, however, and the Harbour Commissioners banned the practice. Schools were provided in Dalkey for the children of the workers. Parents paid a fee of 2d. per week per child to attend, about one cent in today's money. But food costs were high and workers complained that "lodgings or rooms are double price to any other county". Prices had soared, even higher than in Dublin, because Dún Laoghaire was becoming a boom town.

Many of the families lived in "courts". These were the filthy backyards of houses and shops along Dún Laoghaire's main streets. They lived in primitive sheds and huts, without any sewers and often without a water supply. Where there were outside pumps, the water was often contaminated by sewage and this caused disease to spread. Nearly a third of the population of the town lived in about 140 courts. When the harbour neared completion and the demand for labour fell, there was no place for these workers to move onto. Their situation grew more desperate.

Monkstown resident, Charles Haliday, campaigned on their behalf. He was also the author of a survey on the appalling sewage and water problems in Kingstown. Haliday felt that landlords were exploiting the vulnerable poor, by offering them housing that was in poor condition. There were, of course, no laws then regarding housing standards. It was claimed that a cholera epidemic killed more people in Dún Laoghaire than in any other town in Ireland. This was a result of the dreadful living conditions of the poor. At the same time, very large amounts of money were spent on developing "an esplanade for the wealthy classes". Haliday himself was to die from disease contracted while visiting the poor.

"In comparatively few of the rooms I visited was there a blanket, the only bed-covering being the clothes worn during the day."

Introduction to the 1867 pamphlet by Thomas Madden

CHECK IT OUT!

- Read *Victorian Dún Laoghaire, a town divided* by Tom Conlon.
- The map above shows three "courts" behind Cumberland Street: Baymount, Molloys and Sextons. Pick out the tiny huts.
- Find out what you can about Charles Haliday and the modern-day school that was his home.

10 cent per day

Workers were paid according to their skill. Tradesmen were better paid than labourers, and the foremen were paid extra. A foreman carpenter was paid the equivalent of 25 cent a day, and an ordinary carpenter 17 cent. Interestingly, a blacksmith earned more. A foreman blacksmith was paid the equivalent of 38 cent a day and an ordinary blacksmith 25 cent. Labourers received much less, as little as 10 cent per day.

While Dún Laoghaire harbour was still being built, its role changed. It had been planned as a place where ships could shelter during a storm or wait to enter Dublin port. But the harbour became much more. Soon it was the leading passenger port in the country and a thriving centre in its own right. By 1911, it was described as "the entrance to the Irish Capital and the Irish Nation."

Much of the credit for this must go to a remarkable man, William Hutchison.

Hutchison was the harbour's first, and longest serving, Harbour Master. He was appointed in 1822 and managed the harbour until 1874 when he retired – at the age of 80! He even lived through the transition from sailing ships to steamships. Hutchison had joined the navy as a boy and had served in the Mediterranean and the Caribbean, reaching the rank of Lieutenant. He was an experienced seaman and he was also a man of great personal courage. In 1829, he was awarded the gold medal of the lifeboat institution for a daring rescue (only four Irishmen have ever received this award). He also took part in the rescue attempt in which Captain Boyd died and was awarded a silver medal by the RNLI.

The new harbour had been designed as an extension to Dublin port. It was not designed for passenger traffic or for importing goods. As a result, it was not equipped with the warehouses and facilities needed. This was to change during the period when Hutchison was Harbour Master.

Coal merchants had been using the small pier (now known as the Coal Harbour) since 1767 to import coal from England. In the 18th century, as many as 40 coal boats were using the pier. But as the population grew, demand for coal also grew (check out the number of chimney pots on the older buildings!). The pier was too small and in 1853 a new pier was built beside it, the Traders Wharf. Large shipments of coal could now enter. It also allowed sulphur and copper to be exported from Avoca and lead to be imported from the Isle of Man.

In 1826, the mail boat transferred to the new harbour. There was no proper place for it to dock, so Victoria Wharf (later called St Michael's Wharf) was built in 1837. In time, this wharf caused problems because it was exposed to the wide harbour mouth in a storm. The Carlisle Pier was built in 1859 and this allowed for the increasing number of passengers disembarking from the ferry.

By the time the harbour was completed, it had outgrown its original purpose. The notorious sandbar of Dublin Bay was no longer the menace it had been. In 1825 the Bull Wall had been extended to match the South Wall and the two walls created a funnelling action in the outgoing tide, which over time scoured away the sandbar. The drifting sand swept around behind the Bull Wall to create Bull Island. At the same time, the new steamships were not as much at the mercy of the wind as the sailing ships. An asylum harbour was no longer urgent.

But by now Dún Laoghaire had taken its own direction. Under William Hutchison, it had become the country's leading passenger port, a commercial trading harbour, a yachting centre and a fishing port. Like Toutcher, Hutchison is a forgotten hero.

CHECK IT OUT!

- Read the poem *Asylum Harbour* by Gerard Fanning.

- Look at a map of Dublin Bay and pick out the South Wall, the Bull Wall and the various piers within the harbour of Dún Laoghaire.

- Find the original Harbour Master's House (now Moran Park House) and the Harbour Commissioners' House.

In 1824, something very curious was towed into Dún Laoghaire. It was a ship without a mast – a "hulk" – and, as onlookers watched, it was moored in the middle of the harbour. This was a prison ship, the *Essex*, and it was to remain there as a chilling presence for the townspeople until 1837.

During the nineteenth century, laws were very severe. More than 100 crimes, some very trivial, could be punished by execution. It was only in 1861 that execution was limited to three crimes: murder, treason and piracy with violence.

From 1821, however, it was common for prisoners to be sentenced to "transportation" instead of execution or a long sentence. They would be "transported" to a distant British colony – often Australia – for a minimum of seven years or for life. It was a way of increasing the population of these lands and it offered free labour to the landowners. Prisoners were often expelled for quite small offences, like stealing potatoes or a sheep to feed their families. Some workers on the new harbour were transported for seven years for stealing on the job! This was the fate of Timothy Hanlon who in 1840 was convicted of stealing a chain and tramplate from the harbour.

Prisoners who were sentenced to transportation were not sent out in ones and twos. They were held, until there was a full shipload, in a temporary "prison hulk". The *Essex* was originally a US navy ship, captured by the British and used by the Royal Navy.

CHECK IT OUT!

- Read some folk songs about transportation and the modern ballad, *The Fields of Athenry*.

- Find out more about the lives of those who were transported to Australia.

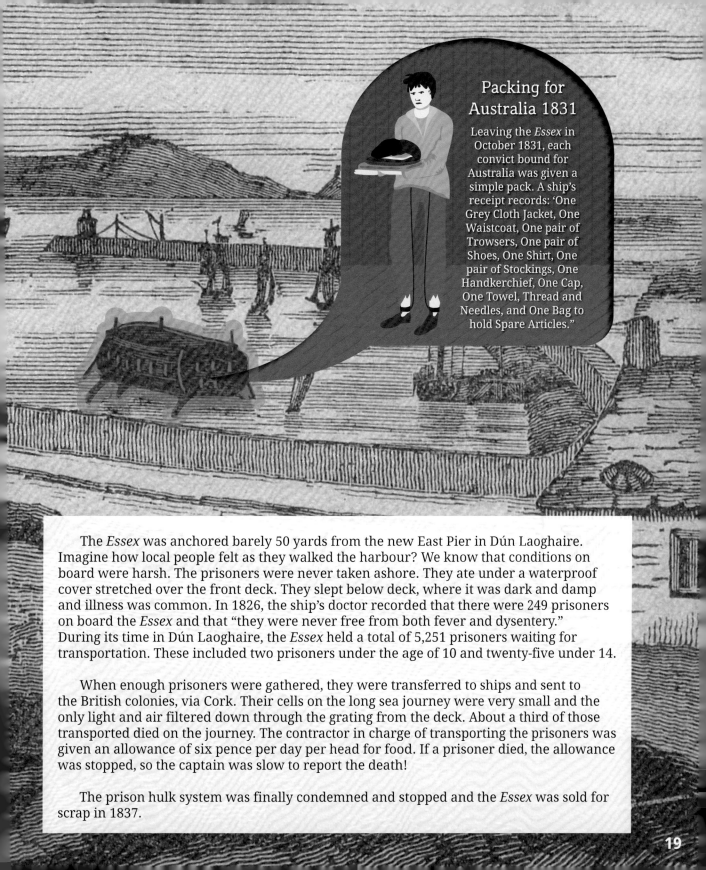

The *Essex* was anchored barely 50 yards from the new East Pier in Dún Laoghaire. Imagine how local people felt as they walked the harbour? We know that conditions on board were harsh. The prisoners were never taken ashore. They ate under a waterproof cover stretched over the front deck. They slept below deck, where it was dark and damp and illness was common. In 1826, the ship's doctor recorded that there were 249 prisoners on board the *Essex* and that "they were never free from both fever and dysentery." During its time in Dún Laoghaire, the *Essex* held a total of 5,251 prisoners waiting for transportation. These included two prisoners under the age of 10 and twenty-five under 14.

When enough prisoners were gathered, they were transferred to ships and sent to the British colonies, via Cork. Their cells on the long sea journey were very small and the only light and air filtered down through the grating from the deck. About a third of those transported died on the journey. The contractor in charge of transporting the prisoners was given an allowance of six pence per day per head for food. If a prisoner died, the allowance was stopped, so the captain was slow to report the death!

The prison hulk system was finally condemned and stopped and the *Essex* was sold for scrap in 1837.

A New Town Grows

At first, there was a tiny fishing village called Dunleary. One writer called it the "dirty abode of a few fishermen, in the bottom of a valley." This village was in a creek, near the spot where the Coal Harbour is today. Passengers from ships entering Dublin often took refreshments at the Coffee House on the hill above. In 1815, barely 300 people lived in Dunleary but by 1851, the population had exploded to 10,453!

What happened to attract such a flood of people?

Most of all, it was the building of the new harbour. Workers flocked in their hundreds, bringing their families – by 1823 there were more than 800 working in the quarry or in the harbour. They needed food, clothes and supplies and traders soon followed, selling their goods. Dunleary also began to attract wealthy families. Some saw it as a better place to live than in the city. Dublin was a very unhealthy place with poor sanitation and great poverty and many children died young. People felt much safer by the sea.

So, the town grew.

By 1840, the village had become a town and the centre moved east along the line of today's George's Street. Some existing buildings date from this time – the Harbour Master's house, the Harbour Commissioners' House, the Royal Marine Hotel and two of the sailing clubs. A local resident, Charles Haliday, described a "small town which can be walked from one end to the other in an hour, with some of the wealthiest people in Dublin." It was now the main passenger port for Ireland.

The name of the town changed. When King George IV set sail from the harbour in 1821, Dunleary became Kingstown to mark the event. It kept this name until 1920, when the town was re-named Dún Laoghaire.

Kingstown became a very fashionable place to live. City people loved it too and took the new train from Dublin for day trips by the sea. They walked the East Pier, listened to concerts, watched boats sailing in the summer regattas or swam and caught the last train home. Not so very different from today! Later, however, there was another reason to visit Kingstown – the Pavilion, a vast entertainment palace by the sea.

But the greatest stir was caused by royal visits. As the royal yachts entered the harbour, ships fired gun salutes and huge crowds gathered on the shore. Queen Victoria visited Kingstown several times. When George V landed in 1911, they needed eight vans to carry his personal luggage into Dublin!

However, there was another side to Kingstown. Behind the wealth and behind the fashionable streets, many people lived in very poor conditions. Charles Haliday campaigned fiercely on their behalf and wrote about the shocking living conditions of the poor.

"A town irregularly built, with many handsome terraces, some churches, and showy-looking hotels."

William Makepeace Thackeray, 1843

CHECK IT OUT!

- Read the chapter on 'Kingstown' in *Green and Gold* by Mary Hamilton.
- Find the two monuments which marked the visits of Queen Victoria and King George IV.
- Find more information on the Pavilion and on those who visited it.

The Kingstown Pavilion

It was like a giant conservatory, made of glass and wood, and people walking on the roof felt as if they were walking on the deck of a ship. This was the social centre for the gentry of Dublin. There was a huge hall for concerts and balls, restaurants and four acres of gardens. The Pavilion opened in 1903, was later burnt to the ground and the Pavilion Theatre today remains on the original site.

Ireland's First Railway

At 9am on December 17, 1834, a train steamed out of Westland Row station (now Pearse Station). Every carriage was packed to overflowing with "very fashionable passengers". The train left the streets of Dublin and began to rattle along the coast. Less than twenty minutes later, it pulled to a stop in Salthill, near the old Dunleary harbour. It was an historic day. The launch of the railway had linked Dublin and Dún Laoghaire and marked a new era of transport in Ireland.

The eighteenth century had been a period of canal building and, at first, a canal was suggested to link the new harbour to Dublin. But a group of businessmen (The Dublin and Kingstown Railway Company) campaigned for a railway service. Many worried that a locomotive train would be intrusive, noisy and smoky. But the first such railway was already working successfully in England, between Stockton and Darlington. In 1831 the campaigners showed, through a road survey, the high levels of passenger and commercial traffic between Dún Laoghaire and Dublin. There was, they argued, demand for a railway – and they won.

The railway line was designed by Charles Vignoles and built by William Dargan. Work began in 1833 and was finished a year later, but there were many technical challenges. They had to create an embankment to carry the line across the strand from Merrion to Seapoint and from Seapoint to Salthill. The line also crossed land belonging to wealthy landowners, Lord Cloncurry and Rev. Sir Harcourt Lees, who objected to a very noisy train belching smoke in front of their property. This was solved by tunnelling to hide the train from view and by paying large sums in compensation.

At first, there was only one stop – at Blackrock – but other stations were soon added. The railway line was extended to the current Dún Laoghaire station in 1836. When the Carlisle pier was built in 1859 to dock the mail boat, a track joined the station to the pier.

The railway transformed Dún Laoghaire. It was now a short journey into Dublin and the company was quick to promote the advantages. They built swimming baths at Blackrock which attracted day trippers. But they also promoted the new town as a place to live. Business people could now work in the city but live in Dún Laoghaire, without needing a horse drawn carriage.

But there were casualties too. The railway track embankments changed parts of the coast. In the old Dunleary harbour, the hill where the Coffee House had stood was levelled and the Martello tower, the site of the original ancient fort of Laoghaire, was demolished.

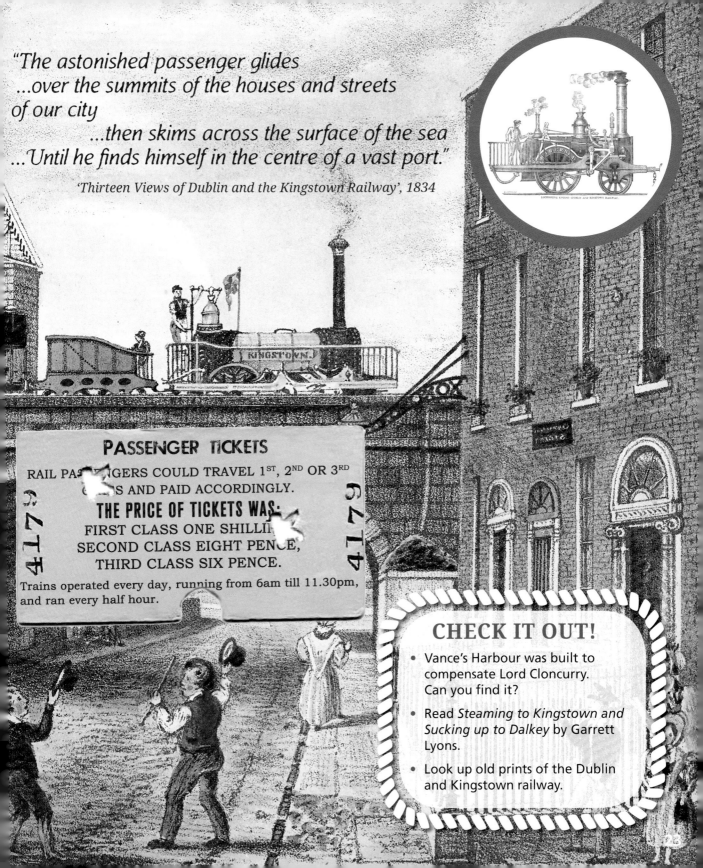

> "The astonished passenger glides
> ...over the summits of the houses and streets
> of our city
> ...then skims across the surface of the sea
> ...Until he finds himself in the centre of a vast port."

'Thirteen Views of Dublin and the Kingstown Railway', 1834

PASSENGER TICKETS

RAIL PASSENGERS COULD TRAVEL 1ST, 2ND OR 3RD CLASS AND PAID ACCORDINGLY.

THE PRICE OF TICKETS WAS:
FIRST CLASS ONE SHILLING,
SECOND CLASS EIGHT PENCE,
THIRD CLASS SIX PENCE.

Trains operated every day, running from 6am till 11.30pm, and ran every half hour.

CHECK IT OUT!

- Vance's Harbour was built to compensate Lord Cloncurry. Can you find it?

- Read *Steaming to Kingstown and Sucking up to Dalkey* by Garrett Lyons.

- Look up old prints of the Dublin and Kingstown railway.

23

The Mailboat and Ferry

It's hard to imagine how important letters were until recent times. Until the later nineteenth century, pen and ink were the only means of communicating and in Dublin people received several postal deliveries a day. In fact, you could send a letter in the morning and have a reply by evening!

As Ireland was part of the United Kingdom, a large number of mailbags travelled across the Irish Sea daily to Britain. In the early days, transporting the mail was the responsibility of the Admiralty and in 1826 the mail service moved to Dún Laoghaire. Every day, the mail boat (or "packet ship") crossed the sea to Britain and eventually there was a complete post office on board. During the sea crossing, post office staff would work below deck, in all weathers, emptying the mailbags and sorting the letters into pigeon-holes.

But in 1835, the mail boat began to carry passengers as well as post. As the new railway was extended, and later connected to Carlisle Pier, the travellers could walk off the train from Dublin and board the mail boat. And from 1848, when trains began to meet the boat in Holyhead, they could travel all the way to London. Each night at 8.45pm, the 'Irish Mail' train left Euston Station in London to meet the mailboat.

"As the train has just come down with its sleepy passengers, and its much more important mail-bags, there is nothing further to delay our departure."

Edward John Hart, taking the Kingstown mail boat, 1895

CHECK IT OUT!

- Find the plaque on the East Pier which commemorates the forgotten Irish.
- Find out more about those who took the Mailboat to England in the 1950s.
- Visit Epic, the Irish Emigration Museum.

By this time, the ship was mainly a passenger ferry but, as the 'Mailboat', it was to be a famous feature of Dún Laoghaire for generations. Until the development of air traffic, it was the main means of travel between Ireland and England. The mail boats took their names from the four provinces of Ireland: the *Ulster, Munster, Leinster* and *Connaught.* Between 1860 and 1920, there were no cross-channel ships in the world to equal them for comfort or speed. In fact, the company responsible for carrying the mail (the Dublin Bay Steam Packet company) was fined for every minute it was late!

For many, unfortunately, the Mailboat was to hold grim memories of emigration. For them, the pier at Dún Laoghaire was a place of heartbreak and loss, particularly in the mid twentieth century when there was great economic hardship in Ireland. During the 1950s, more than 400,000 people left the country, mostly for work in Britain. Many of those who left were hoping for a better life elsewhere and many never returned.

During the better years of the 1960s, a car ferry was introduced at the harbour. At first, each car was lifted onto the boat by crane, but the boat was later replaced by a drive-on ferry. As well as cars, a large number of freight lorries also passed through the port. In 1995, a new passenger terminal was built on St. Michael's Wharf, to accommodate the large Stena Sealink catamaran.

Ferry traffic from Dún Laoghaire across the Irish Sea ended in 2015, when the Stena ferry service was transferred to Dublin port. This brought to an end a tradition that had been closely associated with Dún Laoghaire for 180 years!

The Emigrant Ship

"The weather was bad and my love was sad
As he had to sail away.
He left me here to pine and fear,
Till he'd return some day."

Emigration ballad, 1958

The Worst Storm in Living Memory

On February 8, 1861, Dún Laoghaire experienced the worst storm that anyone could remember. The wind was hurricane-force and made worse by sleet and snow. Slates were ripped from roofs and trees were uprooted. The seas were very dangerous and many ships sank that weekend in the Irish Sea. As the mail boat left the harbour, a massive wave almost sank her and forced her back. The letters being sorted below deck were soaked and had to be dried out on land!

At midday on February 9, the storm worsened and giant waves washed over the piers in Dún Laoghaire. Two ships, the *Industry* and the *Neptune,* were driven onto the back of the East Pier. Captain John McNeil Boyd was captain of the Royal Navy guardship, the *Ajax,* which was anchored in the harbour. He saw what was happening and immediately went to the rescue with 14 volunteers. They tried to help the sailors on board to climb onto the pier, by firing a rocket with a line attached towards the *Neptune.* They were only six or seven metres away but in the terrible gale their efforts failed. Then Boyd and five of the volunteers formed a human chain and waded into the water to reach the crew who were now jumping from the ship. But tragedy struck. A mountainous wave washed the rescuers out to sea. A sixth volunteer was saved: when a wave broke over him, dragging him out to sea, his thumb caught in the rocks! Only one member of the crew of the *Neptune* survived. The captain of the *Industry* lost his life but the rest of the crew were rescued.

The bodies of the brave *Ajax* crew were washed ashore soon afterwards, along with the shirt of Captain Boyd, still with his cufflinks in place! His body was not recovered until two weeks later. The seamen were buried in Carrickbrennan graveyard, Monkstown, where a monument to them and to Captain Boyd was erected. Boyd himself was buried in the grounds of St. Patrick's Cathedral Dublin, where you can find a life-size statue.

The following morning, when the storm had blown itself out, people crowded the seafront in deep shock. The coast of Dublin Bay was littered with masts, pieces of timber and wreckage from the many ships that had gone down in the storm. Twenty-three ships had sunk in Dublin Bay. Thirteen ships were completely wrecked within the harbour and six were lost off the coast of Wicklow alone.

The silver medal for bravery of the RNLI was awarded to seven men including Captain Boyd. A monument on the East Pier marks the place where the tragedy happened and commemorates their sacrifice. A stone lifeboat house was built on the East Pier.

In the 1980s, divers discovered an anchor and the wooden remains of ships in the waters outside the East Pier. Who knows which of the many ships lost in the bay they belonged to? Perhaps even the *Industry* or the *Neptune*.

"Up high upon the mountain waves, were noble vessels tossed, Some were dashed upon the rocks and very soon were lost."

Ballad in the Kingstown Monthly, 1896

CHECK IT OUT!

- Captain Boyd wrote a very popular training manual for sailors. See what you can find out about him.

- Find the Boyd memorial on the East Pier and read the inscription.

- Visit the Old Monkstown graveyard on Carrickbrennan Road and view the memorial there.

The Cradle of Yacht Racing

As large sailing ships filled the new harbour in Dún Laoghaire, another phenomenon also appeared: pleasure sailing.

In 1838, a group of sailing enthusiasts complained that the river Liffey was "every year becoming fouler and less agreeable". Pleasure sailing was not ideal near the busy, commercial port of Dublin. But out in the new harbour it was much easier to get afloat. It was also a short train ride from the city. They established the Kingstown Boat Club which later became the Royal St George Yacht Club. The Royal Irish Yacht Club was founded in the same period and Daniel O'Connell was a member. In 1870, the National Yacht Club was founded. All three remain to this day and are among the oldest yacht clubs in the world. In 1965, the Motor Yacht Club was founded on the West Pier.

The harbour became a centre for yachting, a sport that was spreading around the Irish coast in the nineteenth century. At first, yachting was a sport for the very wealthy. Rich owners of large, ocean-going yachts hired professional crews to do the hard work of sailing. Gentlemen did not do the job themselves. The early boats did not race, instead they carried out manoeuvres in the fashion of the naval fleet. Where they raced, they competed – like horse owners – for large wagers or cash prizes.

Dublin Bay was the birthplace of amateur yacht racing and Dún Laoghaire Harbour was central to it. The founding of the Royal Alfred Yacht Club in 1857 revolutionised yachting – a fact that is surprisingly little known. The club never owned a clubhouse and its members had an unusual goal: to learn "skill in managing vessels". The members planned to sail their boats themselves! They would also race for honour, not money. They drew up rules that came to govern the new sport of amateur yacht racing around the world. They also published the first training manual for yachting in 1873 and started to organise races and regattas in Dublin Bay. Now smaller boats began to fill the seas as amateur yachting took off. Sailing was no longer confined to the very wealthy.

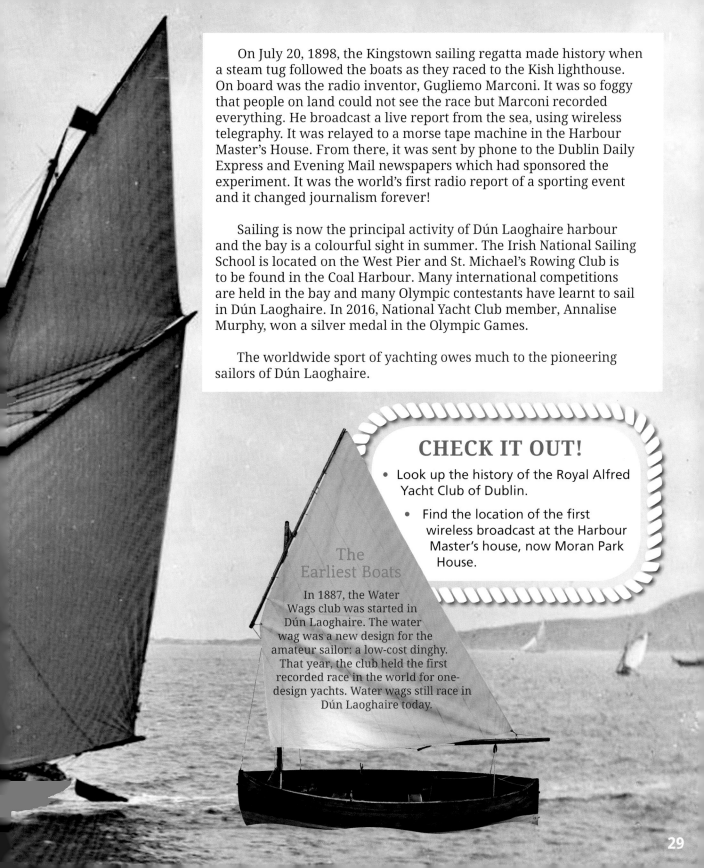

On July 20, 1898, the Kingstown sailing regatta made history when a steam tug followed the boats as they raced to the Kish lighthouse. On board was the radio inventor, Gugliemo Marconi. It was so foggy that people on land could not see the race but Marconi recorded everything. He broadcast a live report from the sea, using wireless telegraphy. It was relayed to a morse tape machine in the Harbour Master's House. From there, it was sent by phone to the Dublin Daily Express and Evening Mail newspapers which had sponsored the experiment. It was the world's first radio report of a sporting event and it changed journalism forever!

Sailing is now the principal activity of Dún Laoghaire harbour and the bay is a colourful sight in summer. The Irish National Sailing School is located on the West Pier and St. Michael's Rowing Club is to be found in the Coal Harbour. Many international competitions are held in the bay and many Olympic contestants have learnt to sail in Dún Laoghaire. In 2016, National Yacht Club member, Annalise Murphy, won a silver medal in the Olympic Games.

The worldwide sport of yachting owes much to the pioneering sailors of Dún Laoghaire.

CHECK IT OUT!

- Look up the history of the Royal Alfred Yacht Club of Dublin.

- Find the location of the first wireless broadcast at the Harbour Master's house, now Moran Park House.

The Earliest Boats

In 1887, the Water Wags club was started in Dún Laoghaire. The water wag was a new design for the amateur sailor: a low-cost dinghy. That year, the club held the first recorded race in the world for one-design yachts. Water wags still race in Dún Laoghaire today.

Lighting up the Coast at Night

> *"On the east pier of Kingstown there is also a light, which revolves and shows a flash every half minute."*
>
> *Sailing directions, 1842*

Every night, lights shine around the coast of Ireland, guiding ships with their flashing signals. Through the darkness, the sailor can find a safe path to harbour. But it was not always so.

Until the nineteenth century, sailing close to the coast or entering a harbour was a time of some risk, especially at night time. It was especially difficult in Dublin Bay, as ships had to find their way through shifting sandbanks and a rocky coastline. Worst of all, there was the dangerous Kish Bank (10km east of Dún Laoghaire) which caused many a shipwreck. The water was so shallow that, in certain conditions, you could stand on top of the bank in the middle of the ocean!

How could they mark out safe passages for ships?

Buoys were already used to mark safe channels, but they were not visible in the dark and they could come adrift in a storm. In some parts of the world, fires were lit to warn sailors of dangers on the coast but something more reliable was needed, a way of permanently lighting the coast. The solution was the lighthouse and, during the nineteenth century, many were built along the Irish coast. Lighthouse keepers lived on site and tended the oil (later gas) lamps and the lenses which magnified the light.

In 1811, to mark the dangerous Kish sandbank, a lightship or floating lighthouse was moored at the bank. She had three lights, a gong which the crew sounded in foggy weather and an 18 pounder gun, which was fired when the mail boat was due. When Dún Laoghaire harbour was built, lights were placed at the ends of both piers and each had a resident keeper.

CHECK IT OUT!

- Visit the National Maritime Museum. See the Wigham exhibition and the huge revolving optic from the Baily lighthouse.

- Look out to the East on a clear day and you can see the Kish lighthouse. At night you will see the light flashing.

The Kish Lighthouse

In 1965, the Kish lightship was replaced by a lighthouse which caused a sensation at the time. It was built in Dún Laoghaire harbour, then towed out to the Kish site, where it was sunk into place.

The tower was then raised to its full 29 metres height through a telescopic action! The beam is visible for 50 km and is now fully automated. You can recognise the Kish by its light pattern: two white flashes every 20 seconds.

In 1853, a disastrous shipwreck near the Baily lighthouse caused a new organisation to be set up. Its role was to light the Irish coasts, to manage the lighthouses and to keep the Irish seas safe. It was to become the Commissioners of Irish Lights and in 1874 a base was built in Dún Laoghaire. It continues its important work from Dún Laoghaire today.

One man was to transform the way lighthouses worked. John Wigham, who lived in Monkstown, was an engineering genius. He invented an oil lamp for buoys which stayed lit in stormy weather. In 1865, he invented the world's first gas-fired light which he installed in the Baily lighthouse in Howth. He also created a revolving lens and was experimenting with electrical lighting at the time of his death.

Lighthouses no longer have resident lighthouse keepers, but are automated. Buoys used today are known as "intelligent buoys" because they not only warn shipping – they also collect weather data and other information.

KISH BANK

"We Save Lives at Sea"

A sudden whoosh and a loud boom. A maroon flare would soar up into the sky and people would know that there was trouble at sea. They also knew that a lifeboat was about to be launched. Today, the call signal is different but the response is still the same. Everything is dropped when a lifeboat is needed. No matter what the weather, a boat takes to the sea and volunteers risk their lives to save others.

Their story of bravery is the story of the lifeboat service in Ireland. For almost two hundred years, the lifeboats have been busiest in Dún Laoghaire and many lives have been saved. But sometimes the boat does not return.

Christmas Eve, 1895, marked the worst disaster in Irish lifeboat history. There was a fierce storm. A ship, the *Palme*, had sailed from Liverpool and tried to shelter in Dún Laoghaire but the storm was so severe that it failed to make the harbour entrance. It dropped both anchors but the cables snapped and it ran aground opposite Blackrock. Two lifeboats were immediately launched from Dún Laoghaire. The larger lifeboat, *Civil Service no.7*, reached the ship first. But as it dropped sail, a giant wave lifted and capsized the boat, throwing the entire crew into the sea. The *Palme* tried to launch its own boat but it was immediately smashed to pieces. The second lifeboat, the *Hannah Pickard*, arrived but this too was capsized by

"If we had been an hour later, I think they would have been gone."

Sam Blackmore, after the 1947 rescue

CHECK IT OUT!

- Find out more about the RNLI and stories of the lifeboat service.

- Visit the graves in Deansgrange Cemetery where the crew of the 1895 lifeboat disaster are buried.

- Find the commemorative plaque on the old lifeboat house near the east pier and the memorial near the George IV monument.

high waves. Luckily, it righted itself but it had to head for shore, having lost half its oars and one of its sails. The crew of the *Palme* was finally rescued two days later, by the Irish Lights vessel, the *SS.Tearaght*.

The entire crew of the *Civil Service no.7* was lost, an event which devastated Dún Laoghaire and is commemorated each Christmas Eve. There is a granite plaque near the old lifeboat house in the harbour which reads, "Their sacrifice is not forgotten."

An historic lifeboat rescue on March 4, 1947, had a happier ending. A fierce gale raged and a Norwegian cargo ship, the *Bolivar*, ran aground on the Kish sandbank. The lifeboat crew was alerted at 4.15pm and, under the command of Sam Blackmore, the *Dunleary II* was launched. The storm was so violent that it took the lifeboat three hours to reach the ship – a journey which should have taken an hour. Despite the mountainous seas, the lifeboat was brought alongside the *Bolivar* from which a rope ladder hung. A female passenger clung to the ladder as the lifeboat was manoeuvred into position and Blackmore yelled "Jump". The passenger jumped and sprawled safely on the lifeboat deck. Over several hours, the boat fought the seas to rescue crew and passengers. All were saved and the lifeboat reached Dún Laoghaire safely at 11pm. Miraculously, the only injury was a broken arm.

There have been lifeboats in Dún Laoghaire since the first lifeboat station was set up in Sandycove in 1813 and later in the old harbour in 1817. In 1861, when the Royal National Lifeboat Institution (RNLI) took over the lifeboat service, a boathouse was built near the east pier (beside the National Yacht Club) and it can still be seen today. The RNLI's mission, "We Save Lives at Sea", continues and lifeboat crews are still volunteers who put their lives at risk. Today, Dún Laoghaire lifeboat is moored permanently in the harbour.

Sunk by a German Torpedo

"I heard this almighty crash and a shattering of glass. I looked into the saloon just before I went upstairs and the whole mantelpiece above the fireplace was fallen down. I got up on deck. Addison, the Second Mate, shouted to me 'We've been torpedoed!'"

It happened on the morning of October 10, 1918. As the mail boat *Leinster* left Dún Laoghaire, it was torpedoed and sank, leaving over 500 people dead. This was the worst ever tragedy on the Irish sea and an event that left families and communities devastated.

It was barely a month before the end of the First World War. The Leinster was leaving the harbour for Holyhead in Wales and, because it was wartime, it was camouflaged. It had only a small gun on board. When it was built, the *Leinster* was the fastest passenger ship in the world. Now it relied on its speed to avoid German submarines lurking in the Irish Sea.

The crew was mainly Irish or Welsh and most of the passengers were soldiers returning from leave. As the boat set off at 8.50am, the postal workers were already working away below deck, sorting 250 sacks of mail. There were 771 people on board. These included 77 crew, 22 postal sorters, 180 civilian passengers and 492 military.

Lying in wait off the Kish Bank was a German U-Boat, SM UB-123, and it soon had the mail boat in its sights. As the *Leinster* passed the Kish Bank, the U-boat fired two torpedoes. One struck the ship in the bow and water started to rush in. The *Leinster* was sinking.

There was a great rush to get the confidential papers out of the chart room in case they fell into German hands. These were to be thrown overboard. An SOS was sent and lifeboats were launched in the heavy seas. But another torpedo struck the boiler room and the ship began to sink rapidly. She finally went under at 10.00 am.

CHECK IT OUT!

- Find the harbour memorial to those who lost their lives in the *Leinster* and see the ship's salvaged anchor above Carlisle pier.

- See the exhibition on the *Leinster* in the National Maritime Museum.

- Find out what you can about submarine SM UB-123.

- Read *The Last Voyage of the Leinster*.

Lizzie Healy

20-year-old Lizzie Healy from Tralee was one of the many passengers who died when the *Leinster* sank. This photo was taken shortly before she made the journey. Her body was brought back to Tralee where she was buried.

There were other ships in the area, but they were ordered not to help for fear of more torpedoes and rescue boats did not arrive for hours. The lifeboats were only designed to hold 53; there were over 70 people in one when a British destroyer arrived to rescue them two hours later.

One survivor described the terrifying scene. "I looked up and saw the foremast crashing down and the fore funnel ripped out, as if by a fellow in a temper. I couldn't wait any longer. I slid over the side. It was quite easy, because she had a good list to port. I slid down and stepped into this lifeboat."

The official loss of life was 501, but more recently we know that 529 people died in the tragedy, many from Dún Laoghaire and Holyhead. The newspapers of the time reported the shocking news of the "ghastly sea scene" and the "harrowing stories." Most of the passengers were soldiers and unfired shells were more recently found in the wreck. But there was no public enquiry and many questions remain unanswered.

Just nine days later, in a sad twist of war, the UB-123 submarine hit a mine and sank. All on board perished.

From Sail to Jet Engine!

For 200 years, ships have entered the harbour mouth at Dún Laoghaire. But over these years they have altered almost beyond recognition. This is because of great changes in ship design and navigation.

When the harbour was built, sailing ships were propelled by the force of wind and tide alone. The more sail a ship had, the faster it went and ships could have up to five masts filled with huge, billowing sails. These ships navigated using a compass and the stars.

During the nineteenth century, the paddle steamer appeared when the coal-fuelled steam engine was developed. In fact, the royal yachts used in the early visits of George IV and Queen Victoria to Dún Laoghaire were paddle steamers. Huge, coal-burning furnaces below deck created the steam that worked the engine. The engine drove a large paddle wheel which propelled the ship forward. This was later followed by a steam engine which drove a propeller and which was much more efficient.

In the twentieth century, there was another great change. Steam engines were replaced by more efficient diesel internal combustion engines. Now a ship might have several engines and propellers, for both speed and safety. The introduction of radar greatly improved navigation.

Finally, the giant catamarans used by Stena Sealink introduced another revolution in ship design. They used the equivalent of jet engines, fuelled by aviation fuel. The most modern ferries are now propelled by similar engines and navigate using GPS.

Sail or Steam?

The change from sail to steam was not immediate. Steamships were expensive to build, coal was costly and ships had to store large quantities of coal on board. But steam won out in the long run, because it was faster and ships could manoeuvre more easily into and out of ports. Now crossing the Atlantic became a journey of a few weeks instead of a few months. This had a great impact on trade and on passenger travel. Shorter journeys meant that ships could carry a greater range of goods. Travel times for passenger ships, such as the mail boat, could be set with great precision.

CHECK IT OUT!

- Study a rigging diagram for a nineteenth century sailing ship.
- Research nineteenth century steamships.
- See the collection of ships' models in the National Maritime Museum.

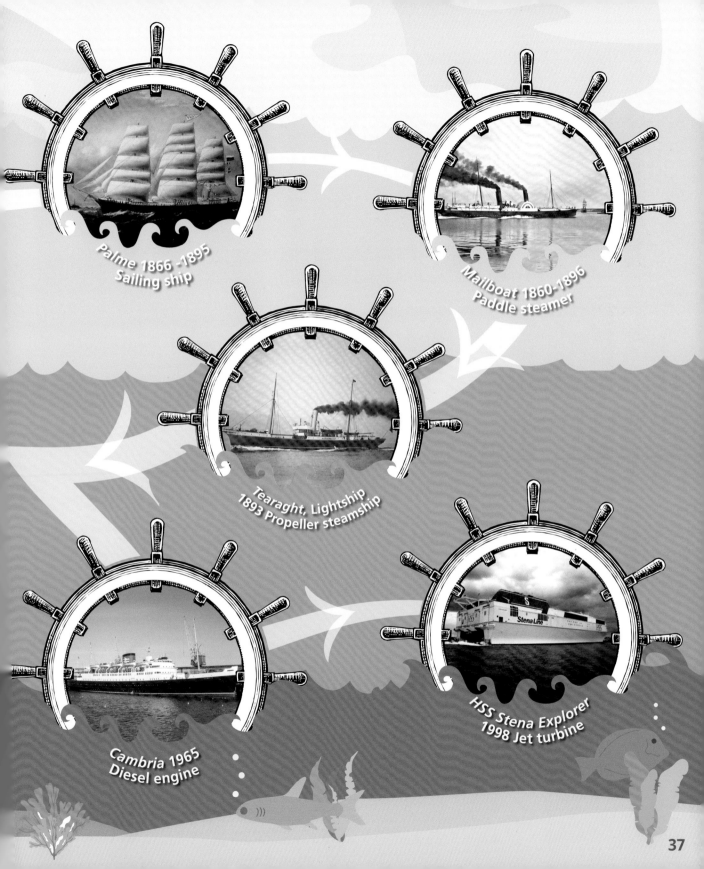

Palme 1866 -1895
Sailing ship

Mailboat 1860-1896
Paddle steamer

Tearaght, Lightship
1893 Propeller steamship

Cambria 1965
Diesel engine

HSS Stena Explorer
1998 Jet turbine

Acknowledgements

I am indebted to several local historians and teachers for their assistance in preparing this text. These include Peter Pearson, Rob Goodbody, Cormac Lowth, Tom Conlon, Seamus O'Connor, Roger Kirker, Maureen Duckenfield, Gráinne Dempsey, Pat Flaherty, Tomás Ó Briain, Donal Ryan and Pat Fox. I am also grateful to Captain Robert McCabe of the Commissioners of Irish Lights and to Captain Simon Coate, Harbour Master, for their advice. I have drawn extensively on the journals of the Dún Laoghaire Borough Historical Society and am particularly grateful to Colin Scudds for his guidance. Dr Marian Keyes and Nigel Curtin of the DLR Lexicon have been of great assistance with regard to the Local Studies resources in the Lexicon.

I would like to thank Dr Susan Gibney and her colleague, Aisling Healy, of Blackrock Education Centre for the opportunity to work on this project. Thanks also to the board of Dún Laoghaire Harbour Company and especially to Gerry Dunne, CEO, and to Carolyn Hanaphy, Commercial Executive.

I would like to express my special thanks to editor, Gráinne O'Malley, and designer, Eliane Pearce, who have engaged with this project with great enthusiasm and skill. It has been my pleasure to work with them.

Any errors or oversights are, of course, my responsibility and I would welcome corrections.

Dr Séamus Cannon.

Images

NLI: National Library of Ireland. RIA: Royal Irish Academy

Cover: Painting by artist Aidan Hickey.
Pg 1. Maps. Dublin Bay c. 1800. Source Peter Pearson; Harbour plan, presumed to be by Richard Toutcher. Source RIA. **Pg 6. A Tragic Shipwreck.** The wreck of the Rochdale. Source NLI; Dublin Bay from Down Survey Atlas of Ireland 1685. Source Blackrock Education Centre. **Pg 8. A Forgotten Hero.** Sailing ships of the nineteenth century. Source Colin Scudds; Pamphlet presumed to be written by Toutcher in 1811, on the need for a harbour at Dún Laoghaire. **Pg 10. "An Able and Intelligent Engineer."** John Rennie. Source Colin Scudds; Aerial photograph of harbour. Source Dún Laoghaire Harbour Company. **Pg 12. Moving a Hill by Rail.** Friction wheel used in raising and lowering wagons of stone. Source NLI; View from Dalkey quarry. Source NLI; Background image of wagons being hauled by horse. Source NLI.
Pg 14. Working and Living Conditions. Background image source Royal Society of Antiquaries of Ireland. **Pg 16. The Harbour Grows.** Background image twentieth century postcard of the Harbour. Source Lexicon; George IV memorial above Carlisle pier. Source NLI.
Pg 18. A Floating Prison. Background image Dublin Penny Journal drawing, showing the prison hulk in the harbour. Source Colin Scudds.
Pg 20. A New Town Grows. Postcard of the Kingstown Pavilion. Source Lexicon; The Dunleary Coffee house c. 1800. Source NLI.
Pg 22. Ireland's First Railway. Dublin and Kingstown Railway, setting out from Westland Row station. Source NLI; An early train, the Hibernia. **Pg 24. The Mailboat and Ferry.** Background image postcard of train and ferry. Source Lexicon. **Pg 26. The Worst Storm in Living Memory.** Background image from Illustrated London News. Source Séamus Cannon; Captain Boyd. Source Colin Scudds; Ajax, the figurehead from Captain Boyd's ship. Source Cormac Lowth. **Pg 28. The Cradle of Yacht Racing.** Background image of yachting in Dublin Bay. Source NLI; Yachting in Dublin Bay. Source Bill Hastings. **Pg 30. Lighting up the Coast at Night.** Background image The Kish Lightship and the Mailboat, painting by Richard Brydges Beechey. Source Commissioners of Irish Lights. **Pg 32. "We save Lives at Sea."** Background image The Kingstown Lifeboat Disaster, the second lifeboat going to the rescue, by J. Nash. Source Séamus Cannon; The old RNLI boathouse. Source NLI; The commemoration ceremony of the 1895 lifeboat tragedy, December 24, 2017. Source Séamus Cannon.
Pg 34. Sunk by a German Torpedo. Background image destruction of a steamer by a German U-boat, WW1, painting by Willy Stöwer. Source Commons Wikimedia; The Leinster alongside Carlisle Pier. Source Seamus O'Connor; Lizzy Healy, who died in the Leinster tragedy. Source Kate Healy Coburn. Among those who died in the Leinster was the widow of Thomas Saunders who lost his life in the 1895 lifeboat tragedy. **Pg 36. From Sail to Jet Engine!** The Palme, shipwrecked Christmas Eve, 1895. Source NLI; The Mailboat. Source NLI; The Tearaght, which ultimately rescued the crew of the Palme in 1895. Source NLI; The Cambria Mailboat and HSS Stena Explorer. Source Justin Merrigan.
Pg 38: Gold medal awarded to William Hutchison by the lifeboat institution, for a daring lifeboat rescue in 1829. Source National Maritime Museum and Roger Kirker. **Pg 40.** Dún Laoghaire Harbour Map. Seal in Dún Laoghaire Harbour, Andrew Wilkinson. 2010. Cormorant Photo by Castlelass at Morguefile.com.

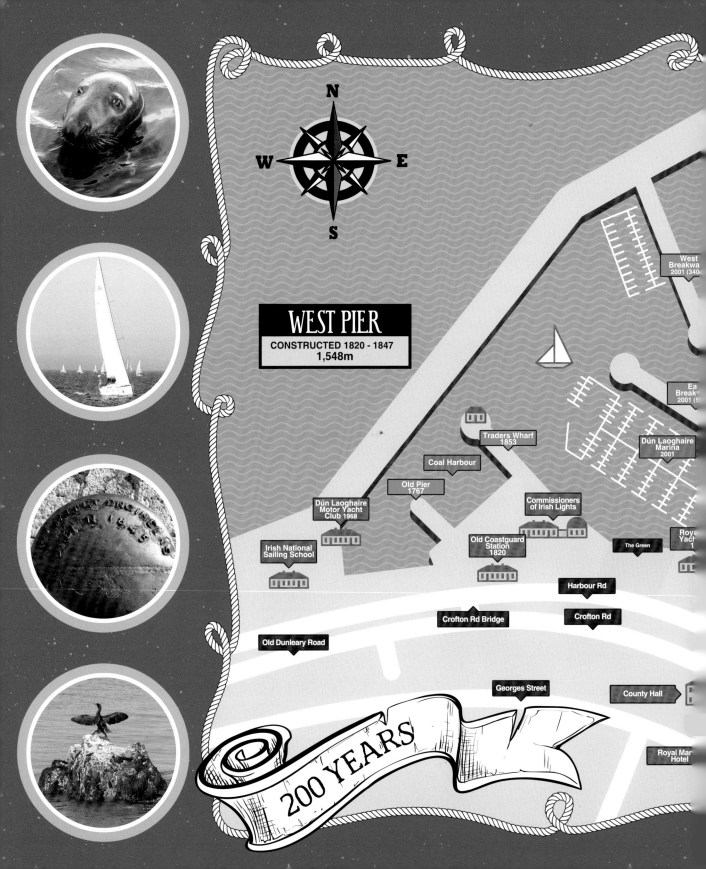

N
W E
S

WEST PIER
CONSTRUCTED 1820 - 1847
1,548m

West Breakwa 2001 (340

Ea Break 2001 (5

Dún Laoghaire Marina 2001

Traders Wharf 1853

Coal Harbour

Old Pier 1767

Commissioners of Irish Lights

Dún Laoghaire Motor Yacht Club 1968

Old Coastguard Station 1820

The Green

Roya Yach 1

Irish National Sailing School

Harbour Rd

Crofton Rd Bridge

Crofton Rd

Old Dunleary Road

Georges Street

County Hall

Royal Mar Hotel

200 YEARS